Where's Mummy Mouse?

T0081359

Ki**m** the **m**ouse lived in a war**m** ho**m**e with her **Mummy**.

They lived underground on a bed of **m**oss.

One day when Ki**m** was asleep, **Mu**mm**m**y **M**ouse left to find food for Ki**m**.

Ki**m** woke up and was scared.

"Where is **my** **M**u**mm**y?" Ki**m** **m**oaned.

Ki**m** left her **m**oss **m**at and went
looking for her **M**u**mm**y.

Ki**m** heard **m**unching behind a bush.

"Have you seen **m**y **M**u**mm**y?" she called.

"No, I haven't seen your **Mu**mm**y**,"
said **M**rs **M**oose.

Ki**m** saw a tail behind a **m**ailbox.

"Have you seen **m**y **M**u**mm**y?" she asked.

"No, I haven't seen your **Mu**m**m**y,"
said **M**iss **M**eerkat.

Ki**m** heard something **m**aking **m**usic up a tree.

"Have you seen **m**y **M**u**mm**y?" she asked.

"No, I haven't seen your **Mu**mm**y**,"
said **M**r **M**onkey.

Ki**m** saw something behind a **m**ound of **m**ud.

"Have you seen **m**y **M**ummy?" she asked.

"No, I haven't seen your **Mu**m**m**y,"
said **M**r Ca**m**el.

"Where is **my m-m-m-m-m-m-M**u**mm**y?" Ki**m** cried.

It was night ti**me** now, and out ca**me** the **m**oon.

"Ki**mm**y **M**ouse!" **M**u**mm**y called.

Ki**m** turned around and there was her **M**u**mm**y, holding a yu**mm**y treat.

"Yay! I found **m**y **M**u**mm**y," said Ki**m**.